FINGERPICKING CHRISTMAS SONGS

Arrangements by Bill LaFleur

ISBN 978-1-4950-6594-1

HAL•LEONARD®
CORPORATION

7777 W. BLUEMOUND RD. P.O. BOX 13819 MILWAUKEE, WI 53213

Visit Hal Leonard Online at
www.halleonard.com

All I Want for Christmas
Is My Two Front Teeth

Words and Music by Don Gardner

All I want for Christ-mas is my two front teeth, my two front teeth, see, my

two front teeth. Gee, if I could on-ly have my two front teeth, then

I could wish you, "Mer-ry Christ-mas!"

1. It seems so long since
2. *Spoken: Good ol' San-ta Claus and*

I could say, "Sis-ter Su-zy sit-ting on a this-tle."
all his rein-deer, they used to bring me lots of toys and can-dy. Gee, but

Ev - 'ry time I try to speak, all I do is
now when I go out and call, "Dan-cer, Pran-cer, Don-ner and Blitz-en," none of them can un-der-

Chorus

whis - tle.
stand me.

All I want for Christ-mas is my two front teeth, my

two   front   teeth,   see,   my   two   front   teeth.   { Gee,   if   I   could   on - ly   have   my
                                                                  { All   I   want   for   Christ-mas   is   my

two   front   teeth,   then   I   could   wish   you,   "Mer - ry   Christ - mas!"
two   front   teeth,   so   I   can   wish   you,   "Mer - ry

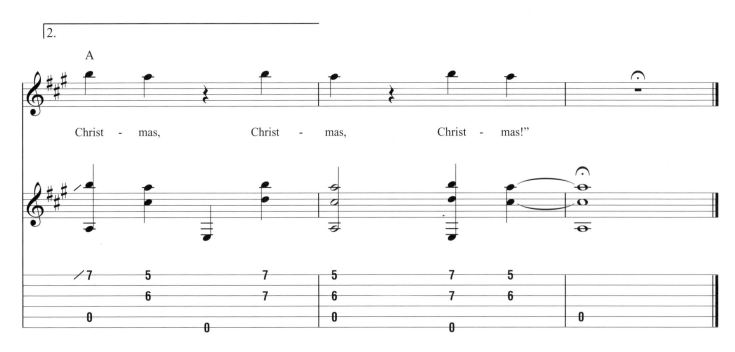

Christ - mas,   Christ - mas,   Christ - mas!"

Baby, It's Cold Outside

from the Motion Picture NEPTUNE'S DAUGHTER

By Frank Loesser

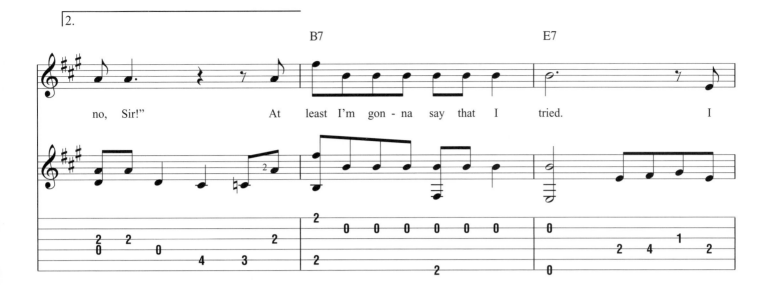

no, Sir!"   At least I'm gon-na say that I tried.   I

real-ly can't stay, _____   ah, but it's cold _____   out -
Oh, ba-by, don't hold _____   out.

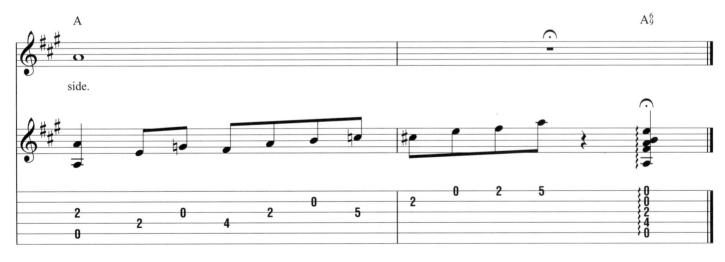

side.

Additional Lyrics

2. The neighbors might think.
   (But baby, it's bad out there.)
   Say, what's in this drink?
   (No cab to be had out there.)
   I wish I knew how to break the spell.
   (Your eyes are like starlight now.)
   I ought to say, "No, no, no, Sir!"
   At least I'm gonna say that I tried.
   I really can't stay.
   (Oh, baby, don't hold out.)
   Ah, but it's cold outside.

Caroling, Caroling

Words by Wihla Hutson
Music by Alfred Burt

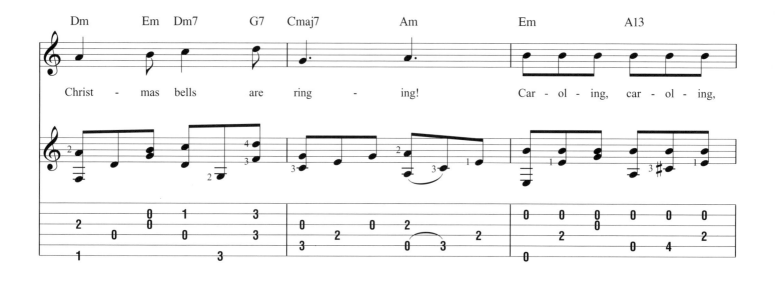

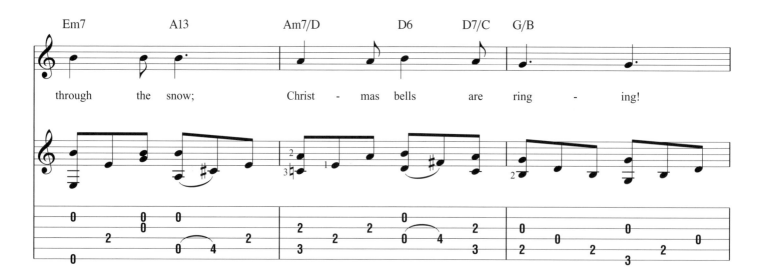

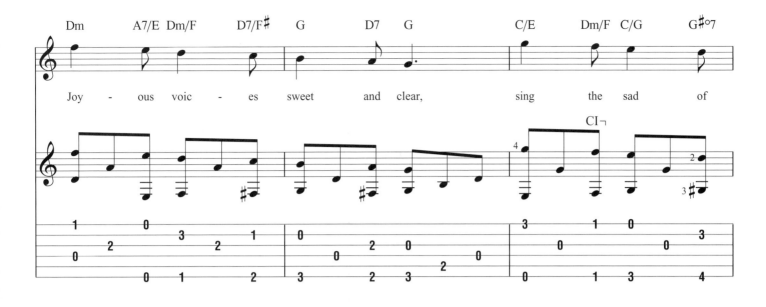

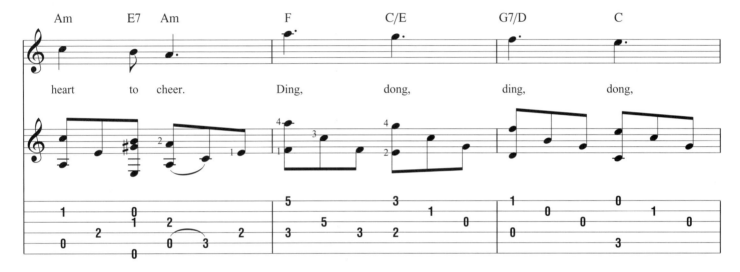

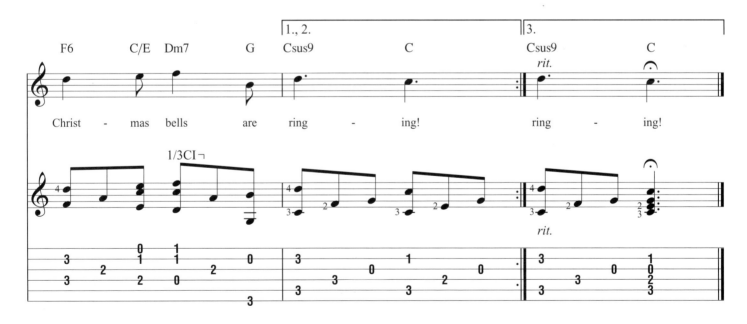

Additional Lyrics

2. Caroling, caroling, through the town;
   Christmas bells are ringing!
   Caroling, caroling, up and down;
   Christmas bells are ringing!
   Mark ye well the song we sing,
   Gladsome tidings now we bring.
   Ding, dong, ding, dong,
   Christmas bells are ringing!

3. Caroling, caroling, near and far;
   Christmas bells are ringing!
   Following, following yonder star;
   Christmas bells are ringing!
   Sing we all this happy morn,
   "Lo, the King of heav'n is born!"
   Ding, dong, ding, dong,
   Christmas bells are ringing!

The Christmas Waltz

Words by Sammy Cahn
Music by Jule Styne

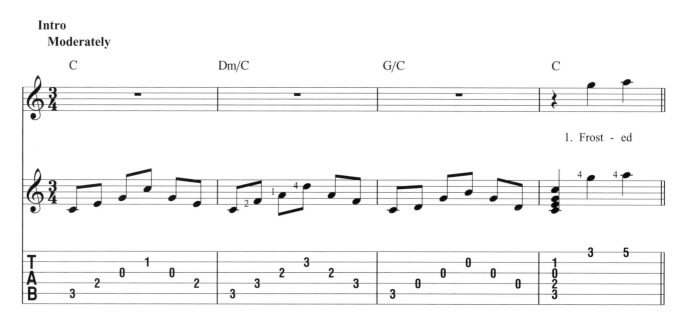

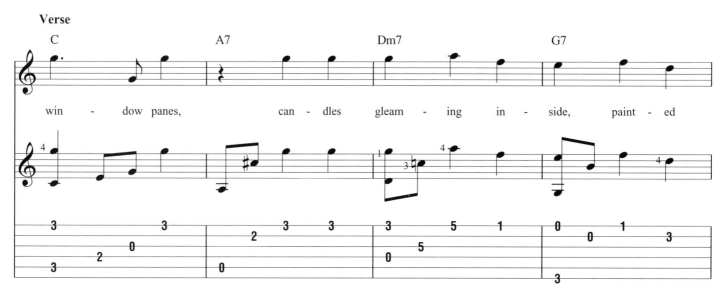

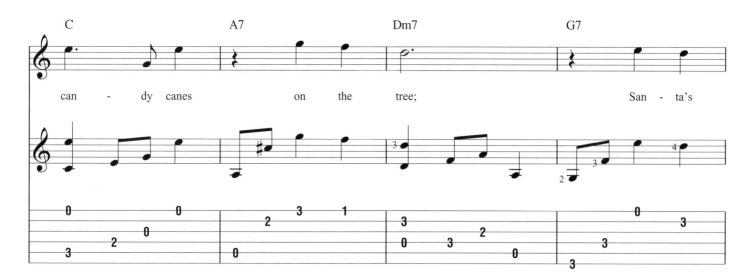

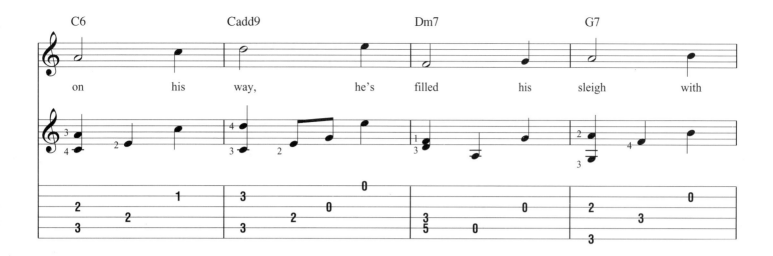

on his way, he's filled his sleigh with

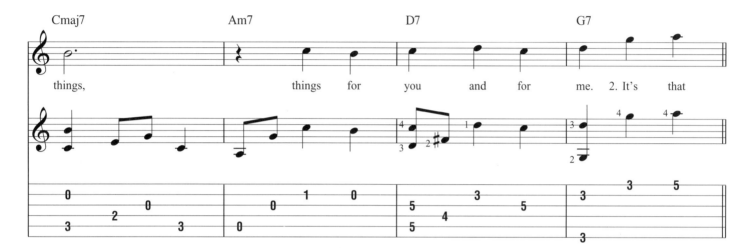

things, things for you and for me. 2. It's that

Verse

time of year, when the world falls in love. Ev - 'ry

song you hear seems to say, "Mer - ry

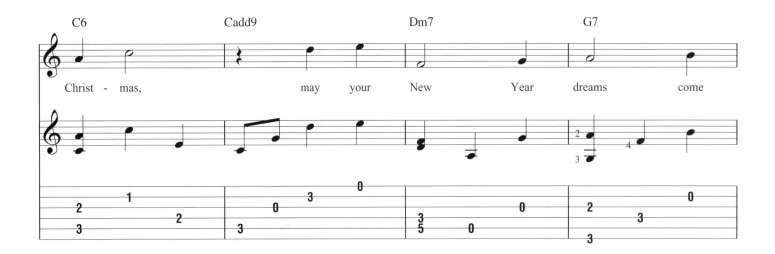

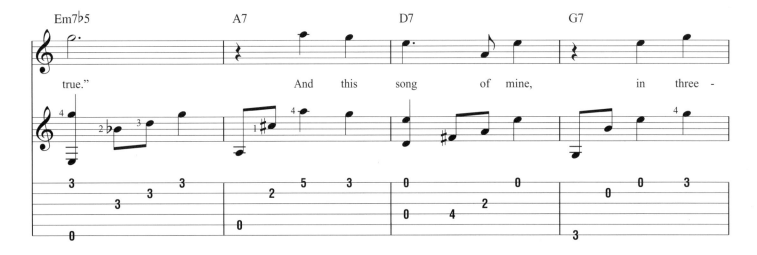

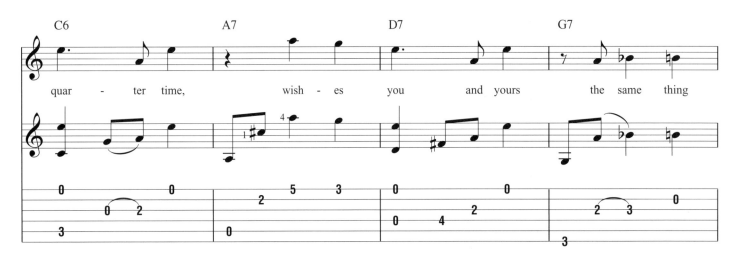

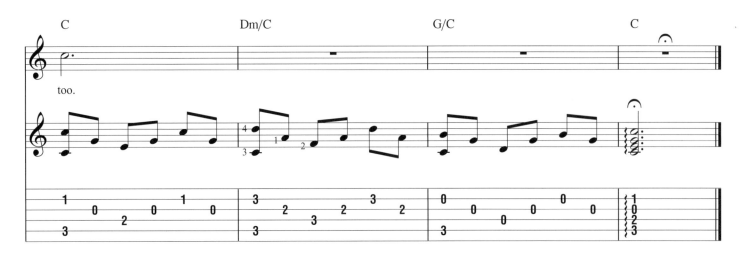

Have Yourself a Merry Little Christmas

from MEET ME IN ST. LOUIS
Words and Music by Hugh Martin and Ralph Blane

Verse
Moderately

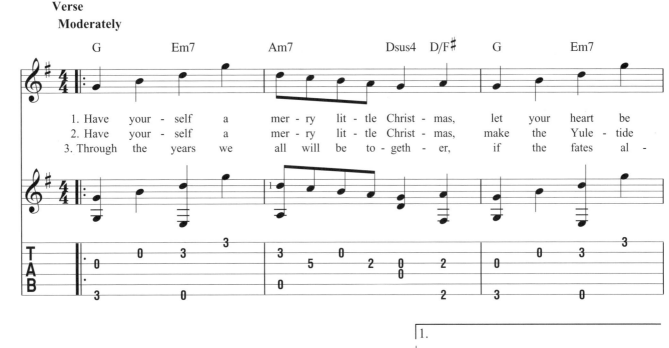

1. Have your-self a mer-ry lit-tle Christ-mas, let your heart be
2. Have your-self a mer-ry lit-tle Christ-mas, make the Yule-tide
3. Through the years we all will be to-geth-er, if the fates al-

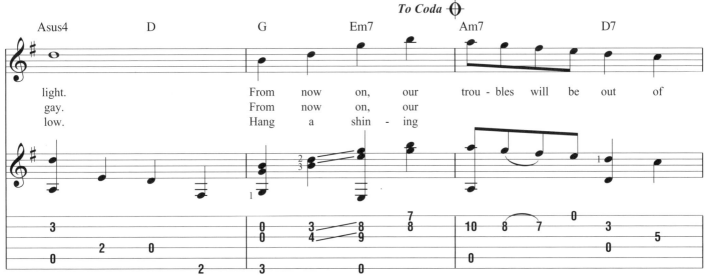

light. From now on, our trou-bles will be out of
gay. From now on, our
low. Hang a shin-ing

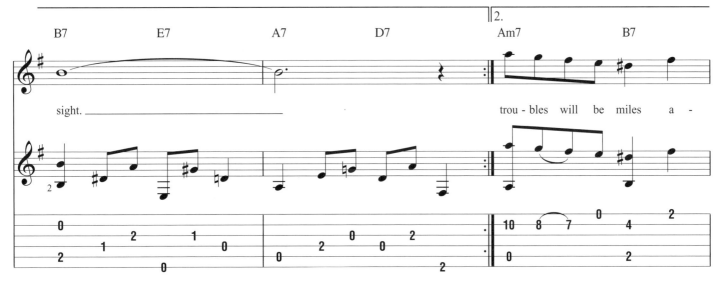

sight. _____

trou-bles will be miles a-

⊕ **Coda**

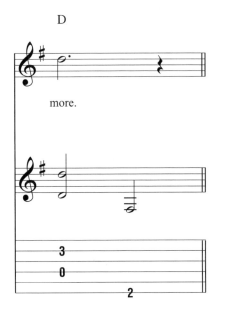

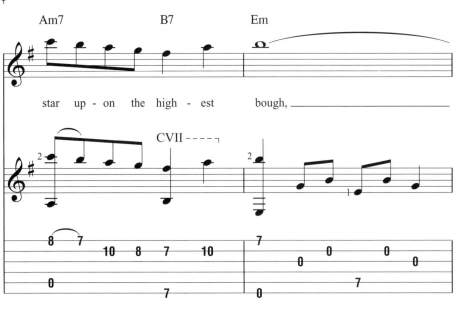

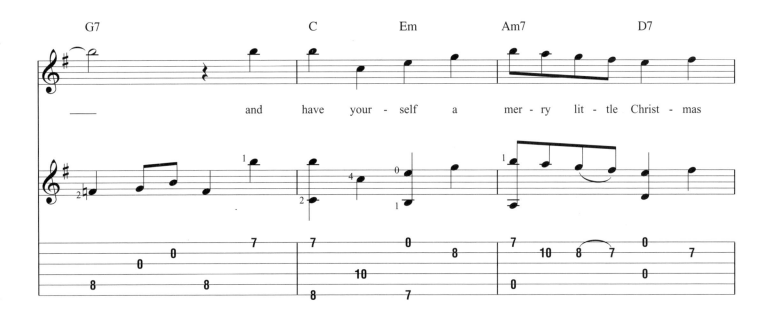

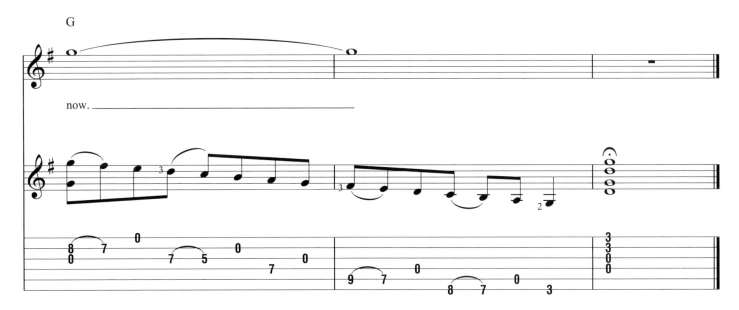

I Heard the Bells on Christmas Day

Words by Henry Wadsworth Longfellow
Adapted by Johnny Marks
Music by Johnny Marks

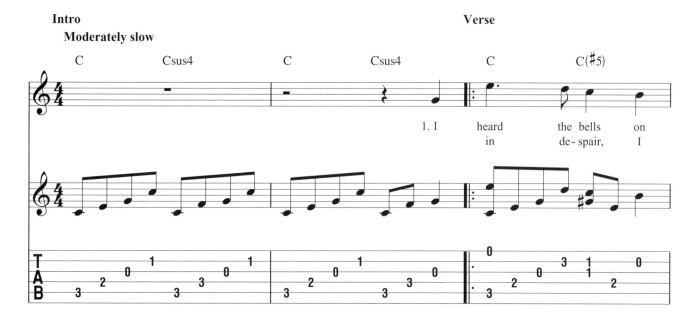

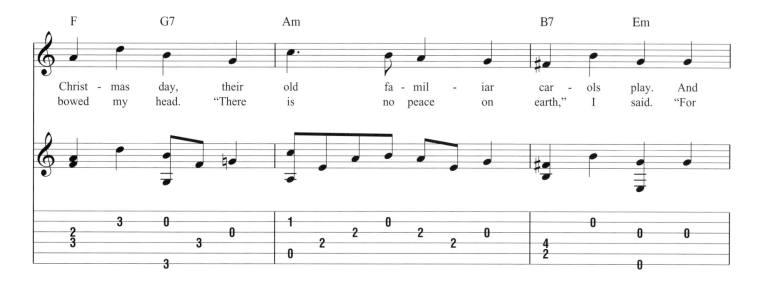

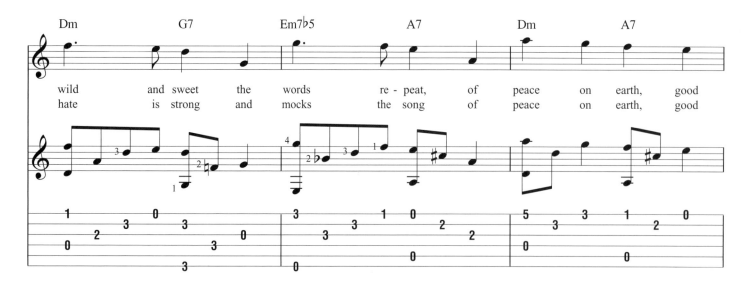

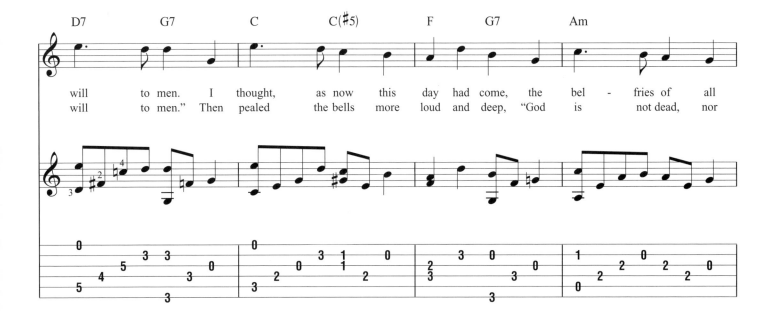

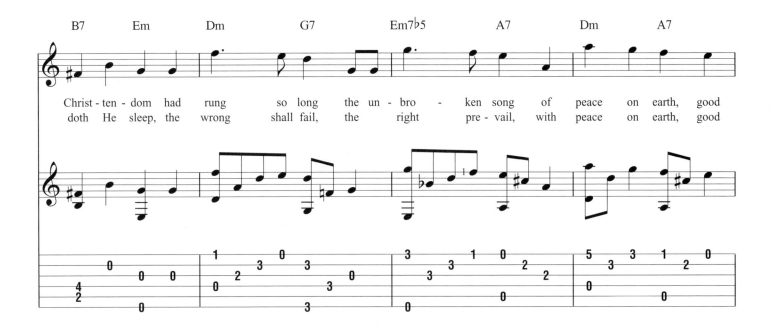

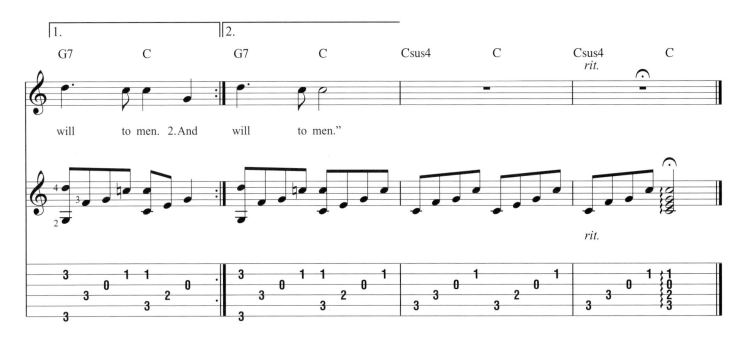

The Little Drummer Boy

Words and Music by Harry Simeone, Henry Onorati and Katherine Davis

Drop D tuning:
(low to high) D-A-D-G-B-E

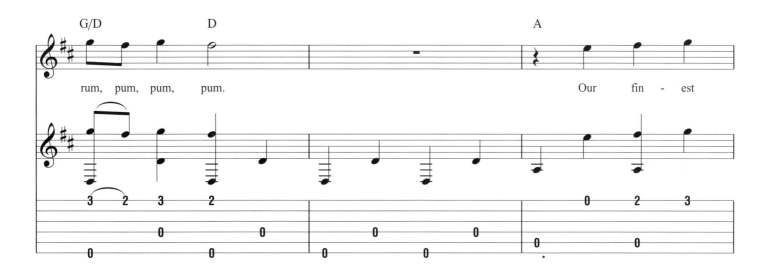

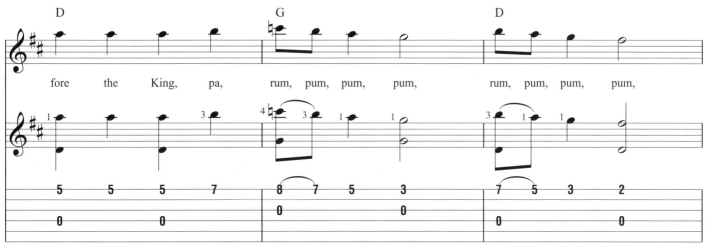

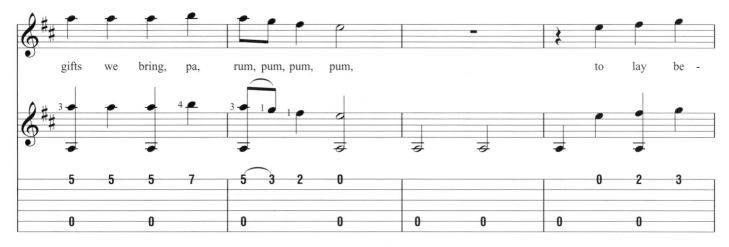

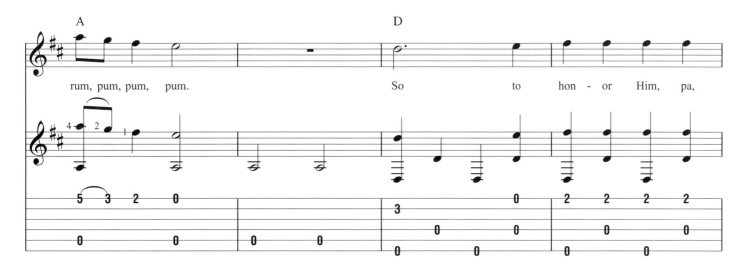

Additional Lyrics

2. Baby Jesus, pa, rum, pum, pum, pum,
   I am a poor boy too, pa, rum, pum, pum, pum.
   I have no gift to bring, pa, rum, pum, pum, pum,
   That's fit to give our King, pa, rum, pum, pum, pum,
   Rum, pum, pum, pum, rum, pum, pum, pum.
   Shall I play for You, pa, rum, pum, pum, pum,
   On my drum?

3. Mary nodded, pa, rum, pum, pum, pum,
   The ox and lamb kept time, pa, rum, pum, pum, pum.
   I played my drum for Him, pa, rum, pum, pum, pum,
   I played my best for Him, pa, rum, pum, pum, pum,
   Rum, pum, pum, pum, rum, pum, pum, pum.
   Then He smiled at me, pa, rum, pum, pum, pum,
   Me and my drum.

A Marshmallow World

Words by Carl Sigman
Music by Peter De Rose

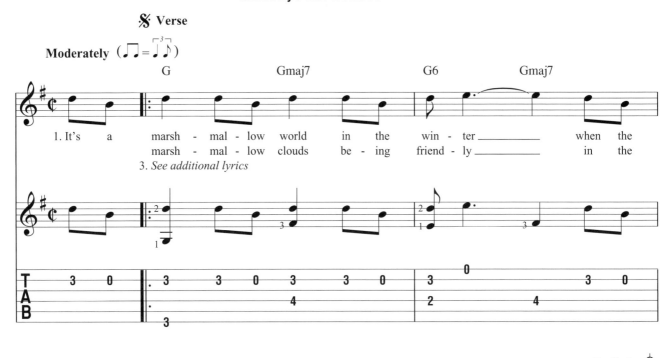

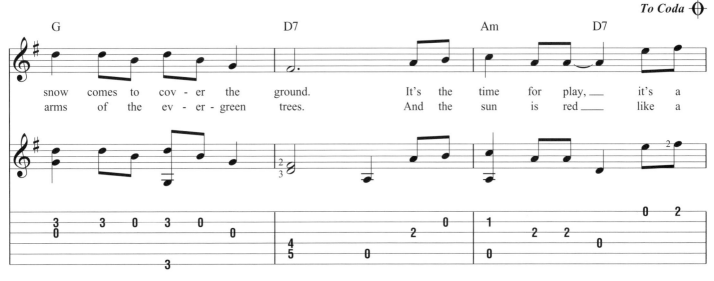

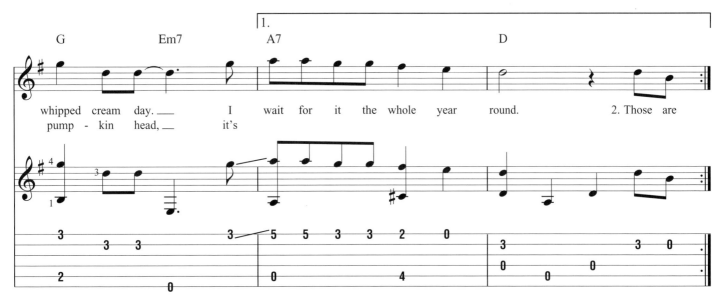

Bridge

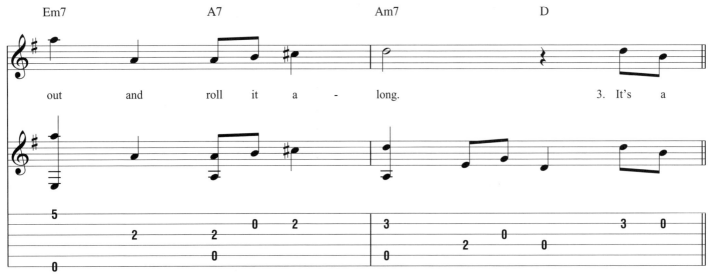

out and roll it a - long. 3. It's a

⊕ Coda

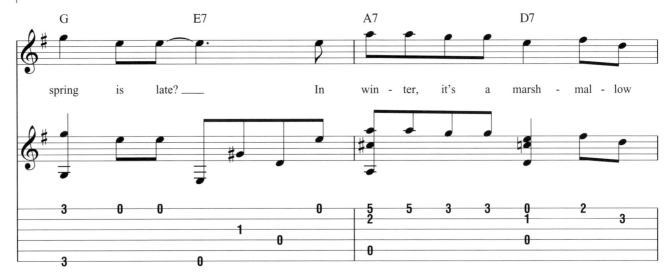

spring is late? ____ In win - ter, it's a marsh - mal - low

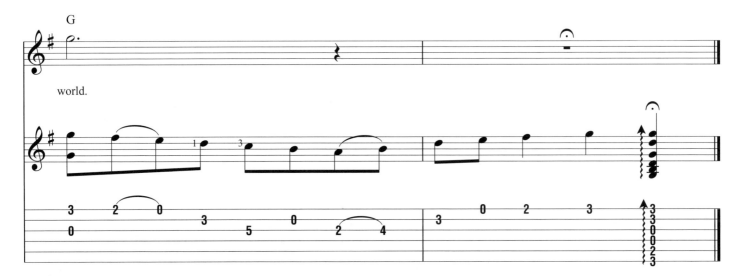

world.

Additional Lyrics

3. It's a yum-yummy world made for sweethearts.
   Take a walk with your favorite girl.
   It's a sugar date.
   What if spring is late?
   In winter it's a marshmallow world.

Mary, Did You Know?

Words and Music by Mark Lowry and Buddy Greene

D.S. al Coda **Coda**

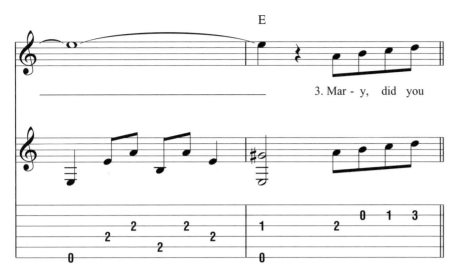

3. Mar - y, did you

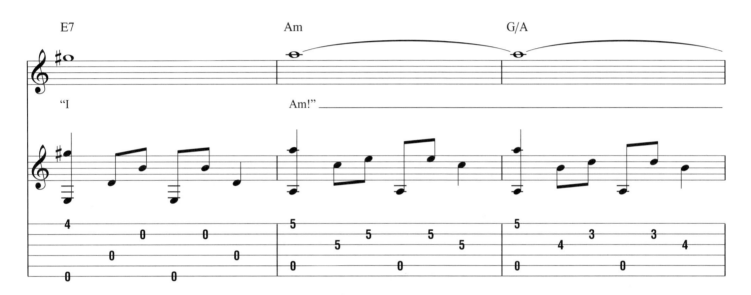

"I   Am!"

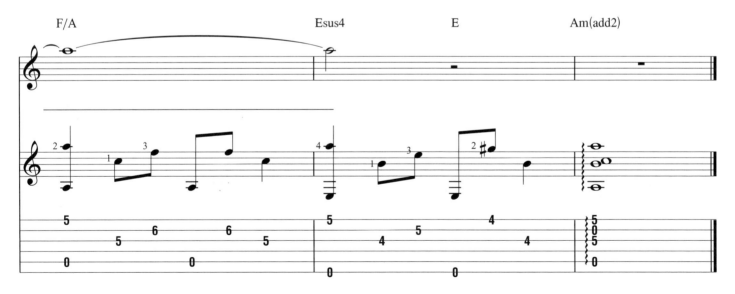

Additional Lyrics

2. Mary, did you know
   That your baby boy will give sight to a blind man?
   Mary, did you know
   That your baby boy will calm the storm with His hand?
   Did you know
   That your baby boy has walked where angels trod?
   When you kiss your little baby,
   You kiss the face of God?

3. Mary, did you know
   That your baby boy is Lord of all creation?
   Mary, did you know
   That your baby boy would one day rule the nations?
   Did you know
   That your baby boy is heaven's perfect Lamb?
   That sleeping child you're holding
   Is the great "I Am!"

Mele Kalikimaka

Words and Music by R. Alex Anderson

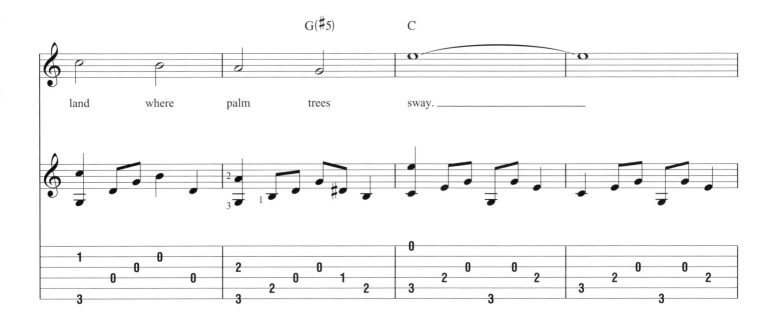

land   where   palm   trees   sway. _____

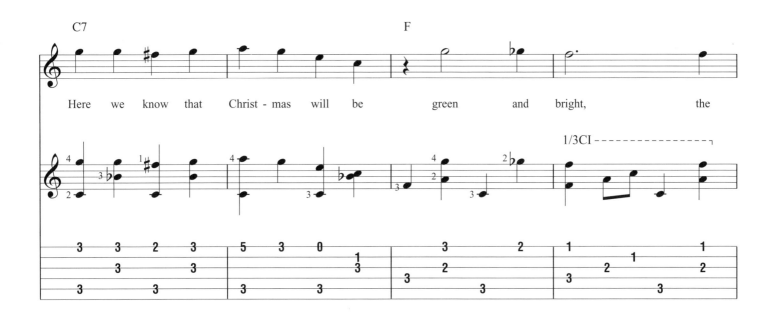

Here   we   know   that   Christ - mas   will   be   green   and   bright,   the

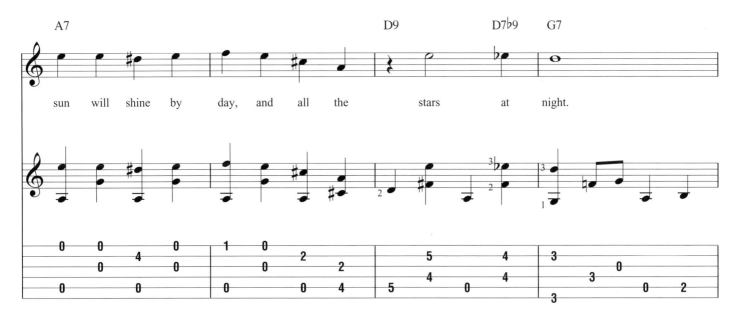

sun   will   shine   by   day,   and   all   the   stars   at   night.

Me - le Ka - li - ki - ma - ka is Ha - wai – i's way to

1.

say Mer - ry Christ - mas to you. _____

2.

you. _____

Silver and Gold

Music and Lyrics by Johnny Marks

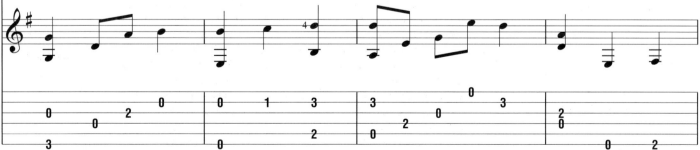

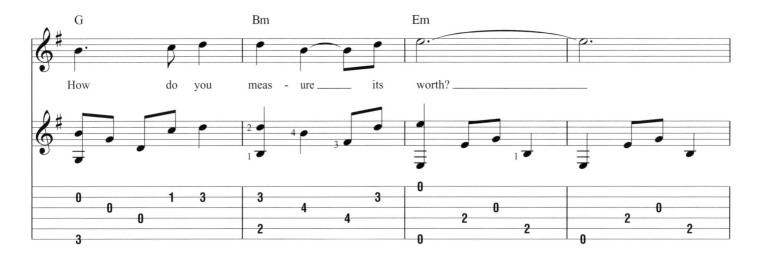

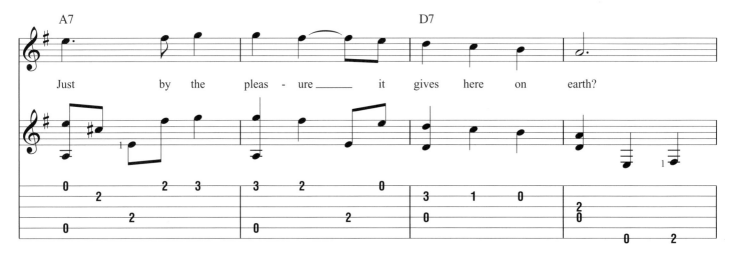

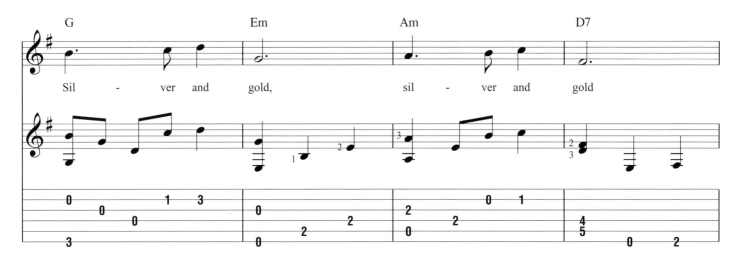

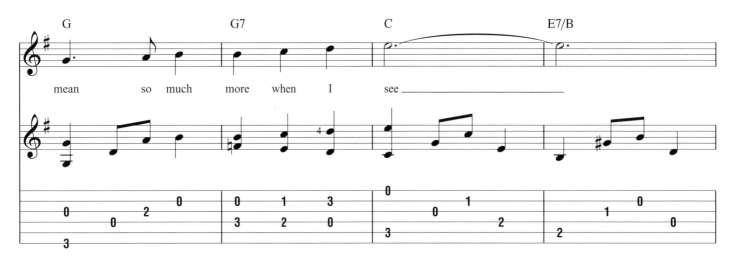

Sleigh Ride

Music by Leroy Anderson

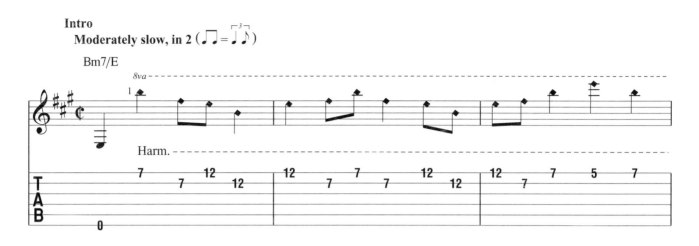

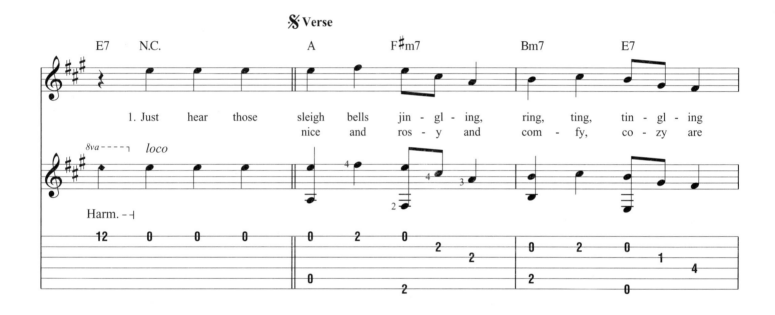

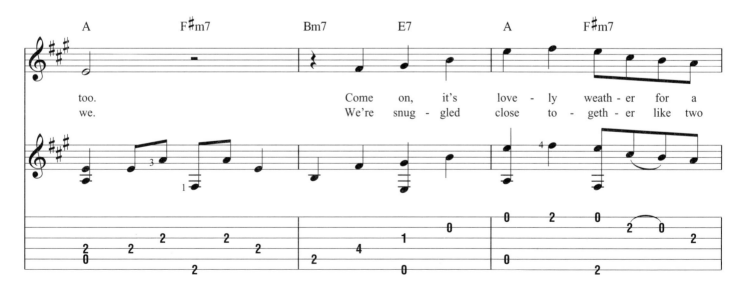

sleigh ride to - geth - er with you. Out - side the
birds of a feath - er would be. Let's take that

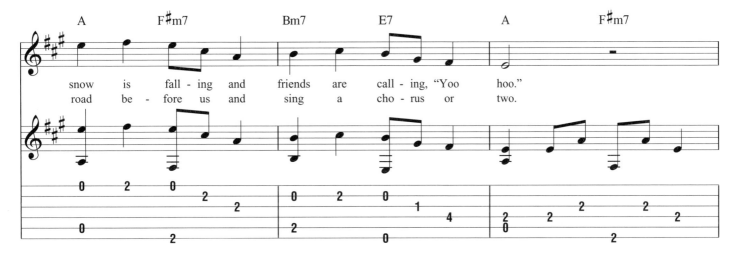

snow is fall - ing and friends are call - ing, "Yoo hoo."
road be - fore us and sing a cho - rus or two.

To Coda ⊕

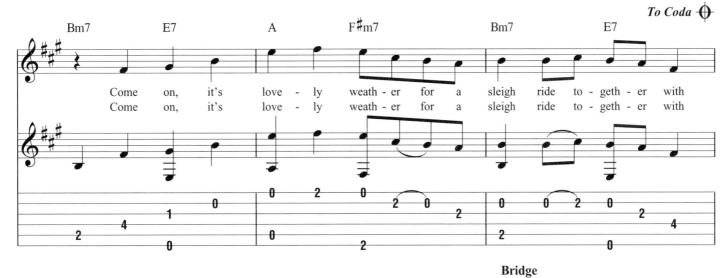

Come on, it's love - ly weath - er for a sleigh ride to - geth - er with
Come on, it's love - ly weath - er for a sleigh ride to - geth - er with

Bridge

you. Gid - dy - up, gid - dy - up, gid - dy -

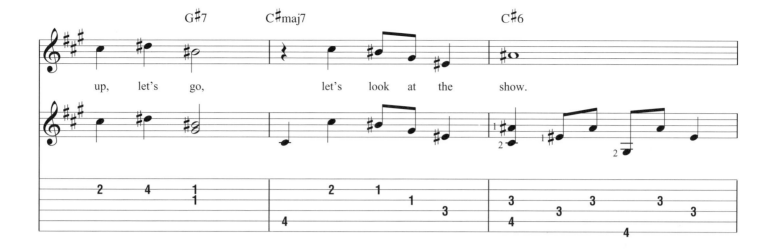

G#7   C#maj7   C#6

up, let's go,   let's look at the show.

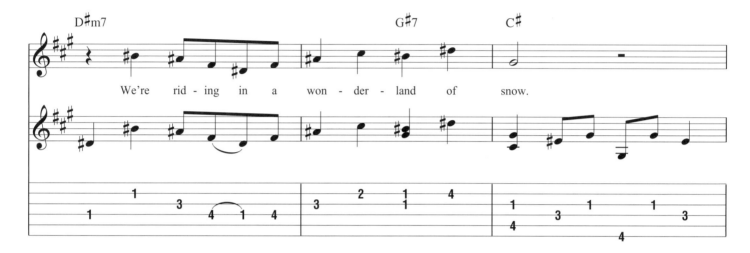

D#m7   G#7   C#

We're rid-ing in a won-der-land of snow.

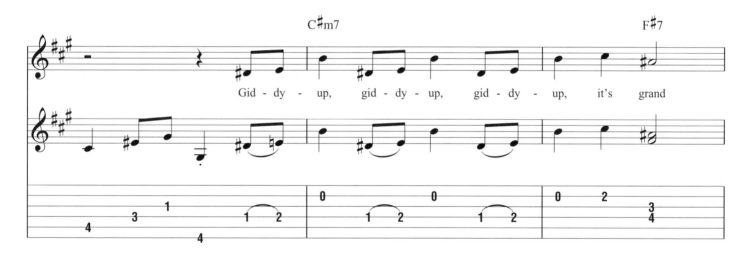

C#m7   F#7

Gid-dy - up, gid-dy - up, gid-dy - up, it's grand

Bmaj7   B6   Bm7/E

just hold-ing your hand.   We're glid-ing a -

long with a song of a win - ter - y fair - y - land. 2. Our cheeks are

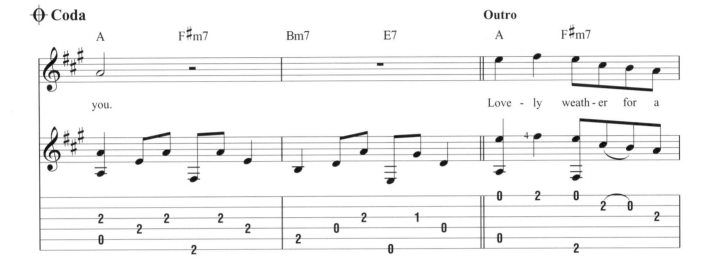

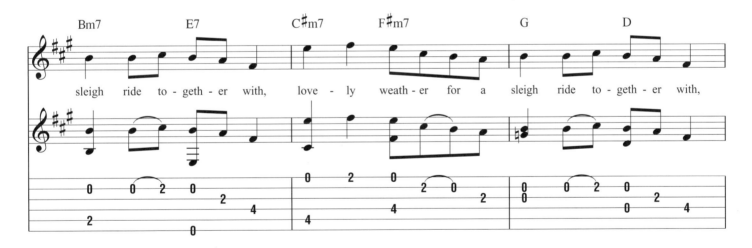

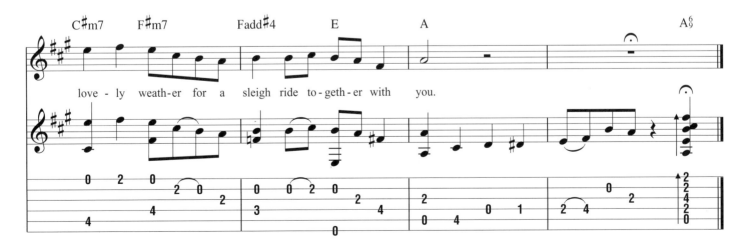

White Christmas

from the Motion Picture Irving Berlin's HOLIDAY INN

Words and Music by Irving Berlin

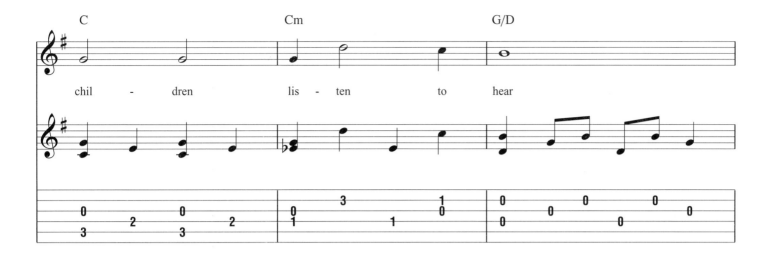

chil - dren lis - ten to hear

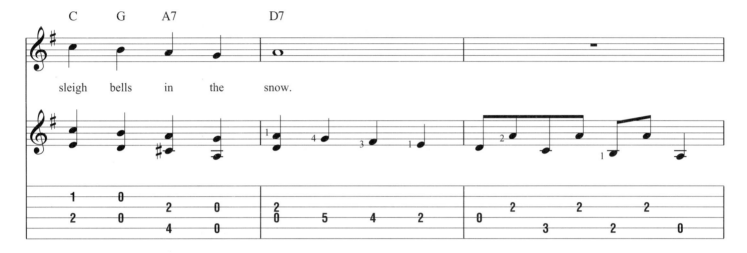

sleigh bells in the snow.

I'm dream - ing of a white Christ - mas,

with ev - 'ry Christ - mas card I write: "May your

Winter Wonderland

Words by Dick Smith
Music by Felix Bernard

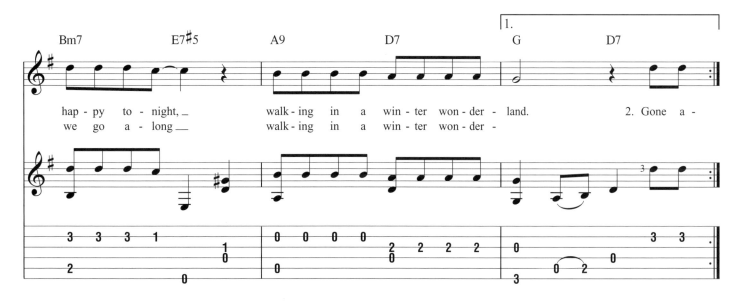

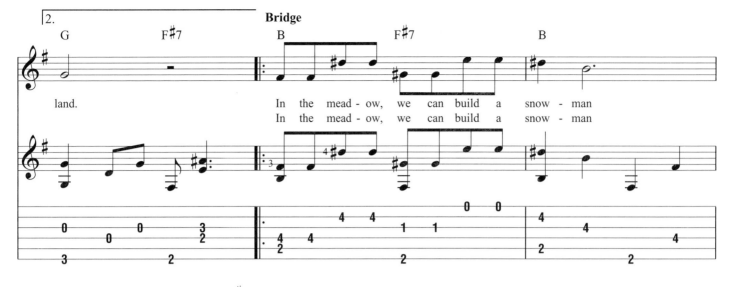

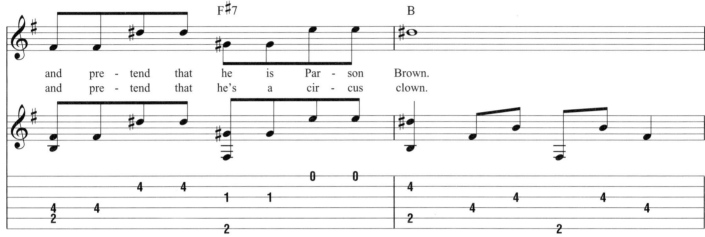

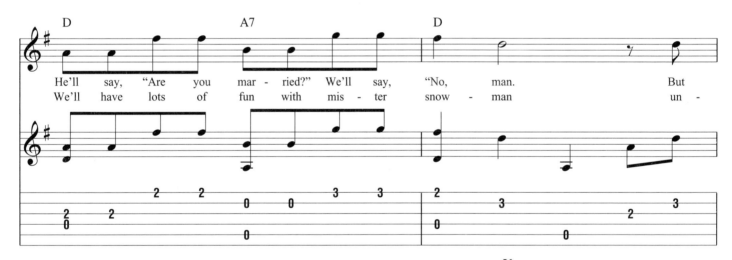

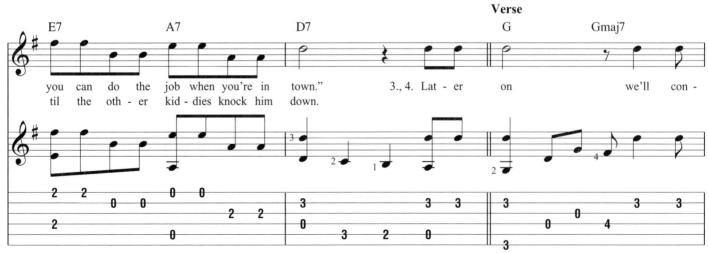

Wonderful Christmastime

Words and Music by Paul McCartney

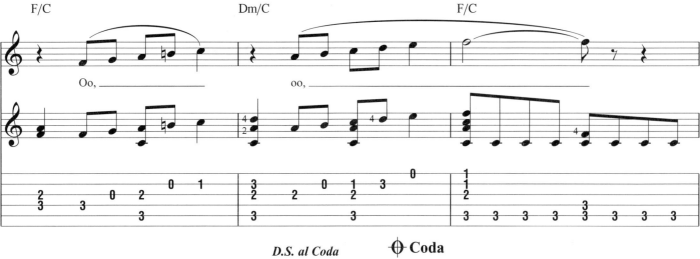

Oo, _____ oo, _____

D.S. al Coda
(take repeat)

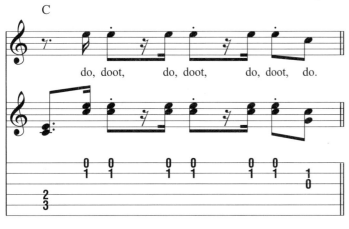

do, doot, do, doot, do, doot, do.

 Coda
Outro

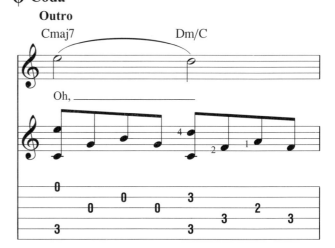

Oh, _____

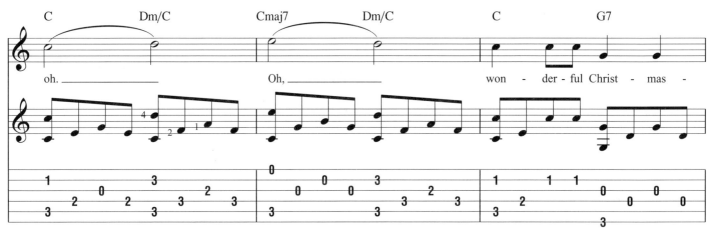

oh. _____ Oh, _____ won - der - ful Christ - mas -

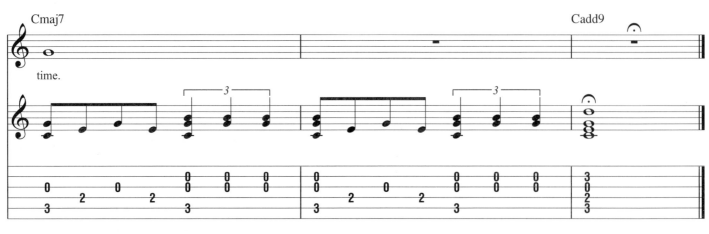

time.

Additional Lyrics

2. The party's on, the feeling's here
   That only comes this time of year.

3. The word is out about the town,
   To lift a glass, oh, don't look down.

INTRODUCTION TO FINGERSTYLE GUITAR

Fingerstyle (a.k.a. fingerpicking) is a guitar technique that means you literally pick the strings with your right-hand fingers and thumb. This contrasts with the conventional technique of strumming and playing single notes with a pick (a.k.a. flatpicking). For fingerpicking, you can use any type of guitar: acoustic steel-string, nylon-string classical, or electric.

THE RIGHT HAND

The most common right-hand position is shown here.

Use a high wrist; arch your palm as if you were holding a ping-pong ball. Keep the thumb outside and away from the fingers, and let the fingers do the work rather than lifting your whole hand.

The thumb generally plucks the bottom strings with downstrokes on the left side of the thumb and thumbnail. The other fingers pluck the higher strings using upstrokes with the fleshy tip of the fingers and fingernails. The thumb and fingers should pluck one string per stroke and not brush over several strings.

Another picking option you may choose to use is called hybrid picking (a.k.a. plectrum-style fingerpicking). Here, the pick is usually held between the thumb and first finger, and the three remaining fingers are assigned to pluck the higher strings.

THE LEFT HAND

The left-hand fingers are numbered 1 through 4.

Be sure to keep your fingers arched, with each joint bent; if they flatten out across the strings, they will deaden the sound when you fingerpick. As a general rule, let the strings ring as long as possible when playing fingerstyle.

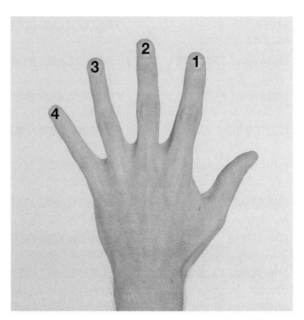

FINGERPICKING GUITAR BOOKS

Hone your fingerpicking skills with these great songbooks featuring solo guitar arrangements in standard notation and tablature. The arrangements in these books are carefully written for intermediate-level guitarists. Each song combines melody and harmony in one superb guitar fingerpicking arrangement. Each book also includes an introduction to basic fingerstyle guitar.

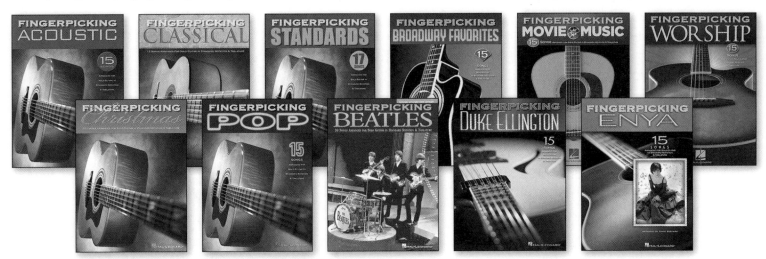

FINGERPICKING ACOUSTIC
00699614...$14.99

FINGERPICKING ACOUSTIC CLASSICS
00160211...$14.99

FINGERPICKING ACOUSTIC HITS
00160202...$12.99

FINGERPICKING ACOUSTIC ROCK
00699764...$12.99

FINGERPICKING BALLADS
00699717...$12.99

FINGERPICKING BEATLES
00699049...$19.99

FINGERPICKING BEETHOVEN
00702390...$8.99

FINGERPICKING BLUES
00701277 ....$9.99

FINGERPICKING BROADWAY FAVORITES
00699843...$9.99

FINGERPICKING BROADWAY HITS
00699838...$7.99

FINGERPICKING CELTIC FOLK
00701148...$10.99

FINGERPICKING CHILDREN'S SONGS
00699712...$9.99

FINGERPICKING CHRISTIAN
00701076 ....$7.99

FINGERPICKING CHRISTMAS
00699599...$9.99

FINGERPICKING CHRISTMAS CLASSICS
00701695...$7.99

FINGERPICKING CHRISTMAS SONGS
00171333...$9.99

FINGERPICKING CLASSICAL
00699620...$10.99

FINGERPICKING COUNTRY
00699687...$10.99

FINGERPICKING DISNEY
00699711...$15.99

FINGERPICKING EARLY JAZZ STANDARDS
00276565 ....$12.99

FINGERPICKING DUKE ELLINGTON
00699845...$9.99

FINGERPICKING ENYA
00701161...$10.99

FINGERPICKING FILM SCORE MUSIC
00160143...$12.99

FINGERPICKING GOSPEL
00701059...$9.99

FINGERPICKING GUITAR BIBLE
00691040 ....$19.99

FINGERPICKING HIT SONGS
00160195...$12.99

FINGERPICKING HYMNS
00699688...$9.99

FINGERPICKING IRISH SONGS
00701965...$9.99

FINGERPICKING ITALIAN SONGS
00159778...$12.99

FINGERPICKING JAZZ FAVORITES
00699844...$9.99

FINGERPICKING JAZZ STANDARDS
00699840...$10.99

FINGERPICKING ELTON JOHN
00237495...$12.99

FINGERPICKING LATIN FAVORITES
00699842...$9.99

FINGERPICKING LATIN STANDARDS
00699837...$12.99

FINGERPICKING ANDREW LLOYD WEBBER
00699839...$14.99

FINGERPICKING LOVE SONGS
00699841...$12.99

FINGERPICKING LOVE STANDARDS
00699836 ....$9.99

FINGERPICKING LULLABYES
00701276...$9.99

FINGERPICKING MOVIE MUSIC
00699919...$10.99

FINGERPICKING MOZART
00699794...$9.99

FINGERPICKING POP
00699615...$12.99

FINGERPICKING POPULAR HITS
00139079...$12.99

FINGERPICKING PRAISE
00699714...$10.99

FINGERPICKING ROCK
00699716...$12.99

FINGERPICKING STANDARDS
00699613...$12.99

FINGERPICKING WEDDING
00699637...$9.99

FINGERPICKING WORSHIP
00700554...$10.99

FINGERPICKING NEIL YOUNG – GREATEST HITS
00700134...$14.99

FINGERPICKING YULETIDE
00699654...$9.99